Platform Papers

Quarterly essays from Currency House No. 14: October 2007

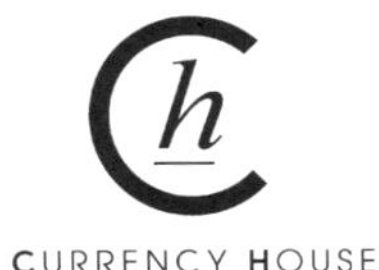

PLATFORM PAPERS
Quarterly essays from Currency House Inc.
Editor: Dr John Golder, j.golder@unsw.edu.au

Currency House Inc. is a non-profit association and resource centre advocating the role of the performing arts in public life by research, debate and publication.
Postal address: PO Box 2270, Strawberry Hills, NSW 2012, Australia
Email: info@currencyhouse.org.au Tel: (02) 9319 4953
Website: www.currencyhouse.org.au Fax: (02) 9319 3649
Executive Officer: Polly Rowe

Who Profits from the Arts? Taking the Measure of Culture

ISBN 978 0 9802802-4-1
ISSN 1449-583X

Cover design by Kate Florance
Typeset in 10.5 Arrus BT
Printed by Hyde Park Press, Adelaide

This edition of Platform Papers is supported by donations from the Keir Foundation and individual donors. To them and to all our supporters Currency House extends sincere gratitude.

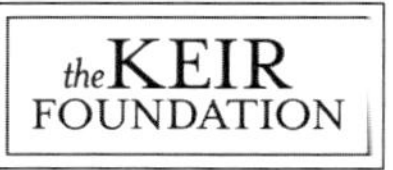

Contents

AVAILABILITY *Platform Papers*, quarterly essays on the performing arts, is published every January, April, July and October and is available through bookshops or by subscription. For order form, see page 72.

LETTERS Currency House invites readers to submit letters of 400–1,000 words in response to the essays. Letters should be emailed to the Editor at info@currencyhouse.org.au or posted to Currency House at PO Box 2270, Strawberry Hills, NSW 2012, Australia. To be considered for the next issue, the letters must be received by 12 November 2007.

CURRENCY HOUSE For membership details, see our website at: www.currencyhouse.org.au

Who Profits from the Arts?

Taking the Measure of Culture

KAY FERRES
and
DAVID ADAIR

The authors

Professor Kay Ferres is a widely published researcher in the fields of cultural participation, aesthetics, creativity and cultural history. She is currently leading *Sustaining Culture*, an Australian Research Council-funded research collaboration involving Griffith University and its industry partners, the Queensland Performing Arts Centre, Adelaide Festival Centre, Sydney Opera House and the Arts Centre in Melbourne. As Dean of the Faculty of Arts since 2003, she currently represents Griffith University on the Arts Queensland Creative Fellowships awards panel and the judging panel for the Queensland Premier's Drama Awards.

Dr David Adair is a researcher who publishes in the fields of cultural citizenship, aesthetics and cultural participation. Since 2005 he has been a Research Fellow in Griffith University's Centre for Public Culture and Ideas, where he works as a researcher and project manager on *Sustaining Culture*. He has lectured in cultural history and in film and media studies at both Griffith University and the University of South Australia, and has also worked in arts media.

Authors' acknowledgements

This essay draws on work we are currently undertaking in the ARC-funded research project *Sustaining Culture: The Role of Performing Arts Centres*. We wish to thank our research colleagues in the project team: Malcolm Alexander, Saffron Benner, Patrick Buckridge, Penny Bundy, Bruce Burton, David Ellison, Nina Gartrell, Louise Goebel, Wendy Keys, Susan Kukucka, Cory Messenger, John O'Toole, and Ian Woodward.

Our industry partners in *Sustaining Culture* are: the Queensland Performing Arts Centre, Sydney Opera House, the Adelaide Festival Centre, and the Arts Centre in Melbourne. *Sustaining Culture* is funded by the Australian Research Council and conducted through Griffith University's Centre for Public Culture and Ideas. We thank our partners, the ARC and the CPCI for their continuing support.

And, finally, we would like to thank John Golder, our editor, and Katharine Brisbane, director of Currency House, for their encouragement and advice throughout the writing process.

1
Vision and Value

Anticipating cuts to the arts in the New South Wales state budget earlier this year, the *Sydney Morning Herald* suggested that the city's star is waning. The Victorian Government's commitment to arts and culture and Melbourne's bid to become a UNESCO City of Literature had attracted comment on the Labour Day weekend. Anne Summers and Andrew Frost both warned that Sydney stood to lose its competitive advantage as Australia's global city. Both appealed to Sydney's sense of itself as edgy, sophisticated and innovative to argue for the importance of investment in cultural assets and resources.

In a piece headlined 'Down South, it's a totally different culture', Summers tallied up Victoria's investment in arts and culture: a $250-million upgrade of the Southbank cultural precinct to include redevelopment of St Kilda Road and construction of a new recital hall; and further development of the State Library, begun by the Kennett government with a $186-million dollar investment, to make it a centre for Books and Ideas.[1] These plans are designed to rebrand Melbourne and add to the 3.5 million visitors who currently attend the venues.

The visionary thinking that Summers applauds links arts and culture with urban amenity and with economic benefits derived from tourism and the attraction of new investment. She reports on her recent visit to Melbourne, and highlights the pleasures of the night-time economy. Invoking the traditional Melbourne-Sydney rivalry, she underscores the value of cultural resources. Melbourne's plans will overcome the disadvantages of 'flat landscape, lack of harbour and inhospitable climate', and the city will overtake Sydney as 'the place to be'. The city's natural resources alone will not be enough to sustain Sydney's position in the global economy.

Andrew Frost pursued a similar tack. His Melbourne visit focused on its 'amazing art galleries and museums' and the 'really good' Federation Square. Sydney comes off poorly in his estimation of cultural value: 'Sydney's public art museums can really compare themselves favourably only to Perth ... or possibly Darwin'.[2] Even Brisbane has invested in culture: the $100-million Gallery of Modern Art might look like 'an inflated beach house', but it is 'actually very nice and the art inside is excellent, too'. Frost's irony transposes to Sydney values traditionally associated with Melbourne. Where the 'grand southern capital' has been transformed, Sydney has become complacent and dull.

Frost's target is leadership. He is critical of leaders in the cultural sector and not optimistic about leadership in politics. While Summers promotes economic benefits, Frost is primarily concerned with the wellbeing of the cultural sector, and with support for contemporary arts. He appeals for 'a bold cultural declaration' regarding the value of arts and culture, but concedes that it is unlikely to come from leaders who believe the arts exist in a sphere apart from other dimensions of social and commercial life.

This tale of two cities raises questions that go to the heart of the research project on which we have been engaged for the last three years, *Sustaining Culture: The Role of Performing Arts Centres*. It is an ARC-funded collaboration between Griffith University and Australia's capital-city cultural Centres: the Sydney Opera House, the Adelaide Festival Centre (AFC), the Arts Centre, Melbourne, and the Queensland Performing Arts Centre (QPAC). Our aim is to produce new research that describes the cultural, educational and economic values of these centres; to develop a more effective language with which to convey the value of performing arts centres; and to devise new strategies for engaging with arts, community, business and political counterparts.

We have one further aim—and we share it with the present series of *Platform Papers*—namely to encourage national cultural debate. So, in the pages that follow we propose to ask a number of important questions: Why build publicly-funded, site-specific arts centres? Why do we hold culture to be a public good? How do we measure its value? Since the 1960s our major cities have competed in the creation of cultural icons worth billions of dollars of investment; and generally the public has endorsed these ambitions. Funding them, however, is quite a different story.

We write from Brisbane, where it is widely believed that Expo 88 has 'matured' the state capital as a city, transforming it from a country town into a vibrant liveable city attracting immigration from the southern states. The Expo site now embraces the major cultural institutions, educational facilities, adapted buildings (some, but not all, with heritage value), commercial and residential development and an urban beach.

Arts and culture are at the centre of this redevelopment. But what does this say about the value of culture, the benefits of cultural participation and the distribution of benefits to a wider community? The enthusiastic adoption of 'creativity' as a cipher for economic development has been driven in Australia as elsewhere by a growing appreciation of the economic value of 'amenity' as well as by the growing market for commercial culture. This work began in the 1950s, but it has recently been boosted by Richard Florida's writings on the 'creative class' (young professionals in high-tech industries) and his work to redevelop cities as 'talent magnets'.[3] Anne Summers cites Florida's influence positively, while at the same time disparaging one of its outcomes: the translation of vision to indicators and measurement.

Florida demonstrated that culture had measurable economic impacts, by linking cultural amenity and quality of life to the attraction of the mobile professionals working in the 24/7 innovation economy. Local populations may not perceive the benefits of the revitalisation of inner cities and infrastructure. The Chaser team's satiric take on the whimsical campaign to promote Melbourne and Victoria as tourist destinations is a reminder that the connection between amenity and economic growth is not apparent to everyone. In the original campaign an unravelling ball of red wool represents the pleasures of discovery for the tourist invited to 'lose yourself in the arts' of Melbourne, but in the Chaser's television parody, locals are caught up in a confusing tangle.

Nevertheless, the work of Florida, and other cultural economists and urban planners, has clearly delineated a new environment for cultural development and arts advocacy: one where government, private enterprise and philanthropy work in partnership, where indicators and measurement inform policy development and where instrumental objectives have dominated the conversation about value. And, as Andrew Frost's *SMH* piece demonstrates, we cannot revert to lofty nineteenth-century ideals about cultural value, much less to modernism's insistence on art for art's sake to justify public investment in the arts.

In the twenty-first century, 'creativity' has assumed a new currency. It has attached itself to technology, to industry and the economy. Where, in this dispersed understanding of creativity, do the 'arts' find a place? Despite the rhetoric about 'creative industries', many arts enterprises are not like industries. Their value is tied to limited production and to distinction. Can the benefits that individuals derive from their participation in the arts be linked to wider social impacts and the creation of public value? The following essay seeks to answer that question.

2

Culture in a weightless world

In the twentieth century, particularly in the era of postwar reconstruction, a public policy focus on nation building rested on a recognition that there are some things that markets cannot supply efficiently. 'Market failure' required public investment in areas such as education, research and development, and the arts. Economists who were the architects of public policy, people like J. Maynard Keynes and Nugget Coombs, could confidently assert that arts and culture were public goods. As Keynes wrote: '[T]he civilizing arts [...] in fact use up an infinitesimal quantity of materials in relation to their importance in the national life and the comfort they give to the individual spirit.' Nor did Keynes believe that the value that attached to enjoyment of arts and culture was only available to the elite. As he saw it, the 'common man's' pleasure in 'ephemeral ceremonies, shows and entertainments' can make him feel part of something more than himself, part of a community.[4]

Neither Keynes's confidence in the public benefits of culture nor his view of markets is so widely shared today. Indeed, the market is now seen to offer answers in many arenas that were once the province of government planning and resource allocation. Confidence in the merits of free markets and the rationality of individuals' choices were at their height in the Thatcher-Reagan era. And they were reflected in the popular culture, notably in Oliver Stone's 1987 film, *Wall Street*. While optimism about market solutions increased, so did scepticism about the value of arts and culture as public goods. Public goods are non-rivalrous and non-excludable, which means that once the benefits exist, everyone can share in them, and one person's share does not diminish anyone else's. With the growth of ecommerce, an increasing number of dispersed niche tastes in books and music can be satisfied by the market.[5] As the products of mass culture became abundant and cheap, the arts have come to signify an elite and expensive taste. A taste for classical music, ballet and opera has increasingly become aligned with the proposition that the 'heritage arts' perpetuate old European values, irrelevant to a population that is increasingly diverse and mobile.

Today, arts advocates are more likely to appeal to the arts' economic contributions to cultural tourism, or else couch civic prestige and aesthetic attainment in terms of the arts' ability to attract capital and a creative and talented workforce to a city or region. Advocates are less likely to resort to an apparently outmoded humanistic consensus that the arts were the finest expressions of the human spirit, with a vital role in improving individuals and society alike. Supporters of the humanist rationale mourn its declining influence, while its critics question its authority and its claim to embody universal values.[6] Explanations for the rupturing of these humanist certainties have included a collapse of the goals of progress that once legitimised support for the arts, increasing competition over resources between a growing number of stakeholders, and rapid changes in technologies and demographics that are altering the ways in which culture is defined, accessed and valued.

Increasingly, governments are reluctant to spend money on 'non-essential' services, and they encourage private investment in such essential infrastructure as telecommunications, health and prisons. Nevertheless, government remains a key player in the provision of cultural infrastructure, whether in the form of the built environment, bandwidth or funding for pillar organisations such as orchestras. And at the local government level, an increasingly important source of funding, culture is an important element of the human and social services that councils provide. It is in this changing landscape that civic leaders have taken a new interest in cultural policy and provision.

As awareness of the economic value of amenity has increased and culture's role in addressing social problems has expanded, local government has emerged as a major supporter of arts and cultural development. It is responsible for the delivery of services to ratepayers and traditionally roads and rubbish collection are deemed to take priority over 'frills' such as cultural programs. Nevertheless, local councils have supported the participatory arts, especially community programs aimed at promoting social cohesion. These range from events celebrating ethnic diversity, to the design of neighbourhoods, to programs for excluded groups such as at-risk youth or the elderly. Councils have also recognised the importance of their cultural assets and have taken opportunities to renew old building stock in order to house studios and galleries and to encourage creative incubators. Place and identity figure strongly in these initiatives.

■

Cultural infrastructure is concentrated in cities, as is the critical mass of human capital that sustains artistic development. Every capital city in Australia now hosts writers' festivals, music festivals and other events in which the arts are set alongside other forms of cultural display. Many of these events are designed to celebrate the diversity of cultures and ethnicities which comprise the modern city and to create new democratic public spaces. Galleries and museums are important civic spaces, mounting exhibitions representing the community to itself as well as to visitors, and providing opportunities for participation in the imagining of civic identities. The town hall continues to be a site of public conversation, often mediated through cultural programs. Suburban libraries are often nodes for the delivery of other council services, and provide venues for community meetings. Performing arts centres, theatres and concert halls are important contributors to the night-time economy, and provide homes for major state-based companies. In addition, these often iconic public buildings symbolise values and achievements associated with knowledge, inspiration and imagination. They are cultural facilities that breathe life into cities, animate public places and contribute to quality of life. Part of their appeal is to the expanding tourist industry, but they are also designed to foster social cohesion and belonging.

What value do cities derive from the arts? This question has been addressed by urban planners and cultural policy makers in the US and Europe over several decades. They have faced challenges of urban decay, the flight of the middle class and the decline of traditional industries. Cultural facilities represent a substantial capital investment and, together with the arts practitioners who work in and through them, are substantial civic assets. They also represent a substantial cost. Few cities have the critical mass of population, visitors and associated markets to derive sizeable, direct, net economic benefits from arts-related activities.[7]

Yet cities have a renewed significance in what the economist Diane Coyle has called 'the weightless world'. They are the focal point of the twenty-first-century global economy, where services are displacing goods as the drivers of value. Industrialisation saw value concentrated in solid objects made in factories on a production line by workers anchored to clock time. Culture, leisure and entertainment were also tied to the clock. The working week of eight-hour days, together with the separation of home and work, shaped the provision of recreation and was reflected in television programming, which segmented the day into family and adult time. In the new 24/7 world, 'dematerialised commodities show no respect for space and geography'.[8]

Cities need to attract human capital to sustain growth. In this environment, new expertise has emerged in research organisations such as Comedia and Demos in the UK, AEA Consulting and Washington's Partners for Liveable Communities in the US. They have long propounded the economic, cultural and social benefits of investment in the infrastructure of amenity. More recently, Richard Florida has emerged as a figure in this advocacy landscape. His study of the 'creative class' demonstrated a positive relationship between technological creativity and cultural creativity (measured by his 'bohemian index', the regional share of artists, musicians and cultural producers). He has developed measures of the attraction of particular locations, using a talent index (level of education), a diversity index (based on gay-couple households), and a coolness index (based on cultural and nightlife amenities and the proportion of population aged 22-27). His finding that low barriers to entry correlate most strongly with diversity and associated values of openness and tolerance underpins his advice to city administrations eager to be 'talent magnets' attracting mobile professionals with high levels of human capital to work in value-added services like finance, software development and biotechnology.

Florida's work is not greatly concerned with what happens in the creative or cultural industries. While he provides a rationale for investment in cultural infrastructure, and for local government to provide support for the creative economy through planning measures such as zoning for cultural precincts, he assumes that arts and creative practice will find their own level in new permutations of cultural production and consumption. In fact, as Adrian Ellis points out, Florida defined the 'creative class' so broadly

> that his theses had little application to the preoccupations of most artists and arts administrators other than to reassure them—if it constitutes reas-

> surance—that they are able to provide some sort of atmospheric background noise to attract computer programmers and bio-technologists to invest in cities like Austin and Seattle with a funky and attractive cultural life.[9]

New technologies are changing the ways in which people connect, share resources and experiences, and value and participate in culture. Information is ubiquitous, accessible and easily reproducible in the weightless world. Diane Coyle argues that value lies in identifying and cultivating the expertise that guides people around this environment of abundance. She quotes Nobel laureate Herbert Simon on resources and scarcity in this world:

> What information consumes is rather obvious: it consumes the attention of its recipients. Hence a wealth of information creates a poverty of attention and a need to allocate that attention efficiently among the overabundance of information sources that might consume it.[10]

Simon's comment, made in 1971, has recently been taken up by commentators on the culture of information technology, who have begun to map out an 'economics of attention'. This work holds out some promise for a new way of taking up the challenges posed to traditional thinking about economics and value by the abundance of mass culture and the blurring of distinctions—between production and consumption, between style and substance, between the real and the virtual, between private and public value. It shifts the old economy's emphasis on productivity and supply to demand for services in the new economy. It also crystallises some key questions: How can arts providers capture scarce attention and provide a memorable cultural experience for new and diverse audiences? How, if at all, do the concepts of cultural capital and 'distinction' apply in this environment?

When complex and creative ideas need to be explored and exchanged, we attach value to interaction. Many interactions can now take place in the virtual environment: work groups can confer, and user groups of one kind or another proliferate. Networks abound. In Europe, where broadband access is not yet universal, about 60 per cent of online consumers are active users of social media, according to a recent Forrester Research report.[11] Face-to-face interactions and social exchanges enhance already existing relationships, instead of always initiating them. Live performance has a new value, but it relies more on synchrony than on co-presence. Global television broadcasts of events such as *Live Aid,* online streaming of *Live Earth,* and virtual-reality worlds such as *Second Life* have changed the nature of 'being there'.

Our research with Australia's performing arts centres addresses questions about cultural value in a networked society. These centres are actively seeking to create public value, to enhance the audience experience and to contribute to a vibrant cultural sector. Strategies to connect with new audiences, particularly young audiences, and to lower barriers to participation are critical to these efforts. As more households are 'wired', and connectivity links home, school and work, expectations of interactivity increase. More and more people manage and create their lives online. The implications for cultural provision are profound:

participation in culture shifts the old lines between producer and consumer.

Performing arts centres may have designs on young cosmopolitan audiences, but these audiences are by no means passive recipients of their attentions. Market research shows that the Generation Y of 18-26-year-olds tends to be highly mobile, with spontaneous social habits and communications preferences that make it hard to reach. Marketing to this demographic requires relatively innovative strategies, such as accessing them through social computing networks, through peer-based publicity that encourages them to participate creatively in the planning and staging of performances, and by generating a 'buzz' through face-to-face publicity, rather than through traditional mass-marketing channels like the popular press. The large performing arts centres also face considerable competition from other kinds of cultural and arts organisations that are better placed to specialise in the kinds of performances and events likely to attract the young and the culturally adventurous. Centres are burdened with conventional auditoria and public mandates to present a comprehensive repertoire. They find it hard to compete with smaller venues that can adapt more quickly to an ever-changing street culture and are thus more likely to provide young audiences with the kinds of benefits they recognise and value.

Melbourne's Arts Centre provides a good example by using its online presence to link into the lifestyles of the young people targeted by the new 'Creative City' marketing campaigns. People in this demographic expect 24/7 access and services; they tend to be rich in leisure choices, but time poor—and they prefer to play an active role in cultural experiences that embrace and move them. The Arts Centre's 'Acts of Creation' website announces itself as a shop window for this young target audience:

> A quiet revolution is taking place in the cultural precincts of Melbourne. Robust, cheeky and fiercely new theatre works are being created with the support of the Arts Centre's FULL TILT and Small Bites! programs. Browse this site and witness some of the artists and ensembles as they undertake the act of creation.[12]

Site visitors can try before buying when they click on 5-minute taster clips from these new productions; they can access news about upcoming events, including workshops run under the FULL TILT program; and they can read about the genesis of each production and view video diaries by their creative teams that give them behind-the-scenes access to the production process. In fact, the site purposely blurs the traditional distinction between producers and consumers: it appeals to 'artists' to submit a proposal, without clearly distinguishing the producer/artist from the consumer/audience. Some of the latter might feel free to adopt the artist persona and take up the site's invitation. This shop window has appeal for many young people, whether they are looking in from a café in one of Melbourne's cultural precincts, their bedroom in a regional town, or a Singapore airport terminal. It is through some of their most personal attributes—their socialising and consumption habits, dreams, ambitions and self-images—that they are connected to each other and to the Arts Centre.

3

Capturing attention

Maynard Keynes understood the individual benefits of the arts as 'the comfort they give to the individual spirit', but he also believed that their 'ephemeral' pleasures afforded individuals a sense of belonging to a wider community. His positive view of the potential social impacts of an individual's appreciation of the arts still has currency in the wider culture. Kay Pollak's Oscar-nominated film of 2004, *As It Is in Heaven,* is built on this premise. A famous conductor takes over a village choir, whose members discover personal courage and social responsibility at the same time as they find their voices. In Ian McEwan's novel, *Saturday*, neurosurgeon Henry Perowne watches his son playing with his band:

> There are these rare moments when musicians together touch something sweeter than they've ever found before in rehearsals or performance, beyond the merely collaborative or technically proficient, when their expression becomes as easy and graceful as friendship or love. This is when they give us a glimpse of what we might be, of our best selves, and of an impossible world in which you give everything you have to others, but lose nothing of yourself. Out in the real world there exist detailed plans, visionary

> projects for peaceable realms, all conflicts resolved [...] But only in music, and only on rare occasions, does the curtain actually lift on this dream of community, and it's tantalisingly conjured, before fading away with the last notes.[13]

Though he has neither Theo's talent nor Keynes's confidence in the idea of community, music is important in Henry's life. It focuses his attention in a way that literature does not:

> Daisy's reading lists have persuaded him that fiction is too humanly flawed, sprawling and hit-and-miss to inspire uncomplicated wonder at the magnificence of human ingenuity, of the impossible dazzlingly achieved. Perhaps only music has such purity. [...] Beyond the arts, his list of sublime achievements would include Einstein's General Theory. [...] Work that you cannot begin to imagine achieving yourself, that displays a ruthless, nearly inhuman element of self-enclosed perfection—this is his idea of genius.[14]

New work about the value attaching to 'attention' does not just take us into the terrain of marketing the arts or getting programming right, but it has reinstated the importance of a rich understanding of what attention means, how it is captured and held, distracted or divided. It also opens up new perspectives on building relationships and understanding how arts and cultural experience connect with personal histories and social networks.

McEwan uses Henry Perowne's appreciation of music as an index of his way of inhabiting the different dimensions of his life and of his connection to the wider world. Michael Goldhaber's developing account of the 'attention economy' has focused on the 'attention transaction'. This is not an exchange based on equivalence, as in the purchase of a commodity. When we 'pay attention', we are creating a different kind of value. In Goldhaber's view, this value has to do with establishing a connection between people.[15] Commenting on his work, John Hagel notes the distinction between the partial or divided attention demanded by multi-tasking and the 'aligning of minds' which characterises close attention: 'Goldhaber's perspective on attention provides an interesting lens to view the distinction between transactions and relationships. [...O]ne important way to amplify the value of attention for all parties is to build relationships.'[16]

This work on attention is more optimistic about the possibility of public benefits deriving from individual commitments than earlier work on cultural capital, which emphasised a hierarchical notion of 'distinction'. Sociologist Pierre Bourdieu's work in the 1960s and '70s was a major influence on many subsequent studies of personal and state investment in cultural capital.[17] These studies were concerned with the means by which cultural consumption reproduces the social and economic status quo; they assumed that 'high culture' was the currency with the highest exchange value, buying social mobility. More recently, Richard Peterson and others have reported a change in patterns of cultural consumption.[18] They distinguish two kinds of consumers: 'univores', who have clearly defined and often singular preferences and use them to establish and maintain exclusive social bonds, and 'omnivores', who sample a wide range of cultural forms and use their interest to connect with diverse social and professional networks. While Bourdieu ties a fixed hierarchy of cultural taste to a hierarchy of social status, Peterson explores a more complex and dynamic world, one where Homer Simpson and the author of *The Iliad* can be appreciated by the same people; where familiarity with Homerisms can be a more socially tradeable form of cultural capital than the Homeric; and where 'univores' create identities around their consumption and tend to form strong bonds, while 'omnivores' with weak ties can more easily socialise across groups.

Some are alarmed by the new cultural pluralism and its social implications; they see it as the dumbing down of culture and blame postmodern cultural relativism and the school curriculum. Others welcome it as a democratic challenge to canonical culture. Whatever the other merits of these public debates about cultural value and the role played by education, they may be missing the point when it comes to the social significance of cultural participation. Television cartoons and classical literature are not appreciated in the same ways or necessarily for the same reasons. Camp, irony and emotion further complicate the picture. An opera buff can have an encyclopaedic knowledge of the art-form and still follow the divas in the music press or in an online community; the same person might also collect action figures and attend *Star Trek* conventions. Opera and 'space opera' do not occupy the same value systems and they circulate in different ways.

Our own research has found that there are many 'omnivores' among the audiences at performing arts centres. Individuals may have cultivated a particular interest in an art-form, say, opera or classical music, but equally enjoy musicals or stand-up comedy. Often they will cultivate those tastes in different ways. One opera lover prefers to see performances alone, and prepares by listening to recordings from his collection in order to better appreciate the nuances of a particular live performance. This close attention is not as important to his enjoyment of a musical. Instead, much of his pleasure comes from the fact that this is an experience shared with his mother, whose own love of music shaped his childhood. A number of our informants recalled a 'magical' moment from childhood when they connected with a live performance, but this was just as likely to have been seeing Humphrey Bear dancing in a shopping centre as attending a performance in a concert hall.

In 2004 we worked with QPAC to conduct a series of focus groups with theatre audiences. One of these groups was made up of Brisbane drama students from a public high school, who had attended a Bell Shakespeare Company production of *The Comedy of Errors*. The students responded enthusiastically to aspects of the show that differentiated it from other stage productions they had seen. They especially appreciated the way the performers stretched the limits of the stage space: characters who confronted members of the audience as the seats were filling up, crossing the lines which define personal space and conventional politeness, and who on stage used highly physical acting styles to cross the boundaries of naturalism. This young audience was aware that their own knowledge of theatre influenced their choices and conditioned their experiences; they understood that as students of drama they had a particular interest in the actors' stagecraft and the director's approach to the production. Their recognition of the variability of cultural capital extended to comparisons of their own reactions with those of older audience members:

> When we were laughing we had older people in front of us who were not laughing—they were not getting the messages. Later they were killing themselves with laughter and we didn't understand that. But not every show has that and I think that was what made it so special as well.

The wider group supported this student's view that the value of the live experience was enhanced by being part of a diverse audience. Though they were on a school excursion to a matinée performance, they did not set themselves apart from the 'grey' audience. Their curiosity about the older audience members' responses to the production might have been the basis of a stimulating exchange, had the opportunity arisen. Our research suggests that modes of participation in the arts are closely linked to the life cycle, to the availability of resources, including time, and the opportunity costs of choices. Once students leave school, they see serious theatre as inextricably linked to the school identities they are eager to leave behind. Their entry into adulthood and independence is supported by different cultural choices.

During a group discussion about the wider social value of the arts, one of the participants spoke—to the approval of the group as a whole—of the value of the performing arts as being 'just variety'; theatre 'is another material medium that you can broaden your mind with, instead of just TV or *Big Brother* or something'. These young theatre-audience members, who would no doubt watch television, were obviously capable of differentiating between these different kinds of cultural experience. Their individual judgements of taste were not entirely 'private', however; in the context of a focus group made up of their peers, they showed that they had learnt to make cultural distinctions in ways that garner social benefits. On this occasion, the speaker's personal taste was validated and the group distinguished itself from those with narrower and less adventurous cultural tastes. Bourdieu used the term 'social distinction' to describe the way in which cultural participation acts as a social gesture, a way of distinguishing oneself from others.[19]

In a focus-group discussion about Bell Shakespeare's trademark strategy of combining set, costume and acting elements from different cultures and historical periods, one participant stated that he and his peers actively sought out challenging cultural experiences:

> People around our age group, or probably a bit older, they are all getting into this alternative arts and they end up getting other people into it, even if you are not that sort of alternative person that likes to go and look at different art, just feeling like something different every now and then.

Unfamiliarity and difficulty, it would seem, do not necessarily act as barriers to induction into a new taste community, especially when an arts education has built up appropriate cultural, emotional and social resources and thus helped bridge the gap. Reinforcing this relationship, so that it does not collapse after the students leave the supportive environment of school, is an ongoing challenge for the arts and education sectors. Nevertheless, as the many contemporary instances of Shakespeare connecting with and being embraced by non-traditional theatre audiences demonstrate, under the right conditions, the unfamiliar can prove attractive. The personal and social rewards of altering one's cultural consumption habits can then act as a salve for any temporary pains of adjustment.

In contemporary culture, the formation of 'identity' has come to be closely linked with the consumption of material and cultural goods. The arts play an important role in connecting this process of identity formation to 'community'. The connection is not always without problems, however; in recent years there have been many examples of how a community founded on identity divides, separates, and helps preserve hierarchies and established networks of power. In extreme cases, where the complexity of these wider associations is denied, the system can lead to 'ethnic cleansing'. We all belong to dispersed groups. Some of these attachments are temporary; some involve formal membership; others depend on processes of mutual recognition. Bonds may be strong or weak, and some memberships intersect. In the case of dispersed groups, habits of participation are critical to their continued existence. The performing arts have a role to play in promoting these habits, including an inclination to cultivate an 'omnivorous' cultural taste.

In the RAND Corporation-financed report, *The Gifts of the Muse*, Kevin McCarthy and his colleagues distinguish private *intrinsic* values (described as the 'missing link' in many rationales for the arts) from public *instrumental* values (in which agendas like crime-reduction or social-inclusion policies are the measure of arts participation).[20] Benefits and values are placed in a continuum, from the most intimate and hard to articulate, to those that are the objects of routine public political debate. The authors' intention in making this fundamental distinction is to make room for less instrumental kinds of participation in discussions on public support for culture and the arts. An ability to distinguish between intrinsic and instrumental values is an important feature of any convincing model of cultural value, yet if such a model is to be comprehensive it must also account for the range of personal, interpersonal and wider social values entailed in cultural participation.

4

Creative choices

Cultural consumption is closely linked to identity and community. It is an integral part of the creation of individual identities. Cultural choices may strengthen the bonds of communities of belonging; they also enable new associations to be imagined.

The wider social benefits of individual participation in the arts has long been assumed; new research is approaching the problem of how to redescribe the arts' private values by unpacking 'the arts' into specific art-forms or disciplines and by distinguishing different kinds of participation. Alan S. Brown and Associates, for example, have developed an 'involvement framework' that uses a matrix of four disciplines—music, theatre, dance and visual arts—and five modes of involvement.[21] These modes are distinguished by levels of creative control exercised by participants, and range from active to passive. Categories do not distinguish levels of professionalism or skill. Involvement in a creative practice is designated 'inventive' and is assumed to be most intense. Interpretive participation is described as 'a creative act of self-expression that brings alive and adds value to pre-existing works of art'; this might include performance or criticism. Curatorial participation—'selecting, organizing and collecting art to the satisfaction of one's own artistic sensibility'—can apply to private or public collections of books, music or art works. Observational participation includes experiences an individual 'selects or consents to, motivated by some expectation of value'. The lowest level of involvement is described as 'ambient', and covers experiences that are not 'purposely selected': this might include exhibition openings, street performances or attendance at events in the company of others. Individuals typically display different levels of involvement with different disciplines.

More recently, Brown has developed a value model (based on *The Gifts of the Muse*) that identifies five clusters of benefits—personal development, human interaction, economic and social, the imprint of the arts experience, and communal meaning—plotted along two key axes: the individual/community continuum and the temporal axis of immediate/cumulative impacts.[22] He also identifies a further dimension of arts participation, distinguishing a group he calls 'initiators'. These are people who introduce others to arts experiences, and who are crucial to any audience development strategy. Taken together, these models identify different aspects of cultural value and provide stakeholders with an integrated map of how they relate to each other. Useful as this map is for plotting forms of participation, the addition of a further dimension—time—would provide a richer picture of involvement over the lifetime of an individual. Aggregate patterns of particular groups would also provide revealing information about choices and the allocation of resources. Brown is by no means alone in working up models of cultural value, of course, but he is worth noting here because he represents researchers who have moved the field along from the earlier intrinsic/instrumental distinctions.

Brown recommends his models to arts administrators as tools for adding value to arts participation, for plotting and extending the links in the value chain. Music CDs, for instance, are revenue raisers for a performer, an orchestra or opera company. They extend the audience members' pleasure and experience; they become part of a personal music library that individuals curate and use, not only to derive satisfaction and pleasure, but to deepen their musical experience and expand their tastes. These supplements can also prompt these curators to seek out other modes of participation—such as attending live performances, enrolling in a class or joining an online chat group—that raise their own levels of creative control. DVDs and books have drawn on this notion of an expanded experience. DVDs frequently make the 'director's cut' available, and include interviews and other supplementary material. Book publishers have long provided such supplementary material in the form of prefaces and critical introductions, but this has lately been extended to include interviews and other notes and questions to guide book-club discussion.

In the UK in 2004, the Department of Culture, Media and Sport funded an initiative, Culture Online, to support projects designed to explore ways in which new and emergent web technology could be exploited to increase democratic participation in culture. A focus on schools was an important part of this effort to expand public access. Funding ceased in 2007, after three years, a timeframe which saw the rapid expansion of internet access in Britain. Many cultural institutions partnered with business and community organisations to explore the potential of online culture and to produce many small-scale innovations. Among the projects funded was the website of Britain's National Theatre, Stagework.[23] This collaboration included theatre companies from across the country, and a technology partner, Illumina Digital. Its first attempt at interactive content featured a scene builder, and allowed users to create their own 'mini production' of Philip Pullman's trilogy of mystery-and-magic novels, *His Dark Materials*.[24] Apart from cutting-edge interactive and multimedia materials, the site includes materials designed to enhance curriculum and learning experiences in a range of disciples, not confined to literary or theatre studies.

■

In Australia, performing arts centres have public mandates to add to the cultural vitality of their states and communities by offering a cultural repertoire that delivers personal well-being and healthy and rewarding social interactions. In a globalising world in which a premium is placed on maximising the personal, cultural, economic and social value of arts activities, the Centres' public role demands that they strike an effective balance between the local and the global. This is as true for cultural and arts organisations such as Britain's National Theatre and Australian performing arts centres as it is for individuals. For organisations it means offering opportunities for cultural participation that promote personal development, cross-cultural understanding, and public trust. The key to their cultural vitality and sustainability lies in the way in which the organisations deliver these services and develop these relationships.

Performing arts centres currently use social and physical spaces to form and maintain certain attributes of their publics. Some of these attributes can be called 'cosmopolitan'. They include capacities for tolerance of the unfamiliar and for adaptability in the face of change, plurality and innovation. 'Cosmopolitanism' is an ethic of world citizenship, a sense of membership in a worldwide humanity and an inclination to draw moral and political imperatives from that affiliation. A cosmopolitan outlook implies a capacity for moderation, an ability to balance the global and the local.

Cosmopolitan people value their affiliations with local and global (or larger) cultures. They are concerned with where the borders between different cultures and art forms are drawn; they not only accept, but derive satisfaction and pleasure from, the fact that cultures are always in flux, are incorrigibly promiscuous, and are constantly giving birth to new hybrids that alter or replace familiar certainties.[25] The popularity of companies such as Bangarra Dance Theatre and Taiwan's Cloud Gate Theatre, and of performers like didgeridoo-player William Barton, demonstrates the growing interest in inter-cultural exchange. Cosmopolitan expectations are that cultures will represent themselves, rather than be represented by others; that when artists invite one another to explore a common ground, they put a positive value on difference and use it to create something new.

Cosmopolitan citizens value a taste for cultural hybridity and a capacity to meet change with equanimity. They look to the arts to foster these attributes and values. In an interview for the ABC-TV program, *Talking Heads,* Australian celebrity cook Stefano de Pieri expressed this trust in the arts' ability to encourage cultural and social mobility:

> Food may be good for the body but we need the arts to nourish our soul as well, and I'm so lucky to have two children who are interested in music, and who have an uncle who is a good musician [and who] is really keen to give them a thorough understanding of music. I believe that without the arts you are not really a complete person. [...] I want them to be engaged with the world; I want them to be modest but authoritative, informed but not arrogant; I want them to be fully grown-up citizens who partake and take responsibility.[26]

If some attributes of cosmopolitanism are invested in the moral personality of the cosmopolitan person, others are found in the policies and interconnected cultural practices and physical spaces where a cosmopolitan ethic is enacted and which give it value as one kind of cultural citizenship among others. Examples of this infrastructure would include the new cultural precincts being developed in cities like Brisbane and Melbourne and the many ways they intersect with the city's art schools, creative industries, galleries and performance venues. These precincts define a new civic space, where all three sectors (public, private and the 'third sector') contribute to the provision of cultural amenity.

The concept of 'community cohesion' is gaining ground in cultural-policy circles where cosmopolitan outcomes are being sought. The more familiar 'social inclusion' concept was a narrowly-focused policy response to the problem of how to deliver social services to the hard-to-reach. 'Community cohesion', by contrast, encodes the cosmopolitan principle of striking a balance between 'valuing diversity, challenging inequalities, and promoting a sense of belonging'.[27] Community cohesion does not assume that affiliation with a specific locality or community takes precedence over or precludes other affiliations. On the contrary, it actively aims to achieve balanced cosmopolitan outcomes. Thus, the British Home Office Community Cohesion Unit defines cohesive communities as those with a sense of belonging *and* an appreciation of differences.[28] The use of community cohesion principles in policy settings encourages heterogeneous and open social networks, in preference to those that are homogenous and closed. This addresses one of the main public-policy issues raised by cosmopolitanism: how best to support citizens as they develop and maintain a range of affiliations.

5

Creating cultural value

The capacity of cultural institutions to secure and maintain public trust is vital to their public role. For galleries and museums, their collections and the conservation of the national heritage are central. The cost and significance of new acquisitions and the sponsorship of visiting exhibitions serve to keep art galleries in the public spotlight. One area of potential conflict, however, lies in the use of public galleries to display private collections on the one hand, and the legitimacy of using this practice to increase the market value of individual works on the other. Performing arts centres also have to maintain a balance among competing responsibilities such as supporting fresh interpretations of traditional forms; encouraging the emergence of new and experimental forms; responding to popular taste, and providing a venue that represents the diverse cultural expression of the local community.

The public for the performing arts is a community of potential beneficiaries. This community is not confined to those who have previously attended a performing arts performance or venue, who currently do so, or who shall in the future. Of course, it is legitimate to talk of specific publics or communities of interest, but 'the public' for the performing arts also includes all those whose lives are in some way touched by them. So measurement of public trust could take account of indicators of the levels of broad society-wide trust in the institution of the arts, or of something more localised, such as expressions of trust in a particular performing arts organisation, event or artist. In each of these senses of 'public trust' we are referring to levels of confidence experienced at either an individual, interpersonal or broadly social level.

There is another sense in which the term 'public trust' is typically applied to the performing arts. This is a 'property held by one party for the benefit of another party'.[29] Such a meaning of 'trust' is most easily identified with the types of state-supported cultural, heritage and arts organisations familiar to Australians, such as the National Trust, the ABC, or state museums and art galleries. Included among these organisations are our large performing arts centres, which receive varying levels of public funding and are typically founded under charters that entrust their boards with delivering products and services to their state-wide communities, audiences and sectors. This meaning of 'public trust' consequently implies an ethic, a way for the organisation to reflect on its public role and act accordingly.

The role of entrusted entity and its concomitant ethic are not limited to state-funded bodies; they are also relevant to charitable and privately-financed cultural and arts organisations that serve the public interest, a service for which the state grants them certain benefits, such as tax exemptions.[30] Commercial activities and imperatives can have a complicating effect on the ability to serve the wider public interest in particular, but these do not in themselves preclude a performing arts organisation, for example, from being entrusted with, or acting in relation to, a conception of the 'public trust'. If it is not the taint of commercial considerations, as such, that impedes an arts organisation in fulfilling this public role, then what does?

In the case of arts organisations receiving significant levels of public funding, the public trust is defined formally, in founding charters and public-policy frameworks. As definers and as guardians of the public interest, governments have mixed expectations, motivations and goals as far as performing arts centres are concerned. They see them as costly public assets whose financial sustainability needs to be secured; they expect them to live up to their charters and deliver comprehensive and exceptional cultural goods and services to the citizens of their states; and they aim to reiterate that a conscious and demonstrable commitment to the public interest is a condition of continued public support.

Responding to these kinds of public expectations can be costly, in both financial and human resource terms. One way for a performing arts centre to spread the costs and risks of innovative responses is by sharing project responsibilities with other parties. A recent notable example involves the Sydney Opera House. The ABC-TV series, *The Choir of Hard Knocks*, broadcast earlier this year, became a hit.[31] Building on the success of *Operatunity Oz*, this latest example of the ABC's 'public interest' take on the reality-television genre continued the earlier series' strategy of forging links between the ABC and performing arts organisations.[32] Viewers of *Operatunity Oz*—which was made in partnership with Opera Australia and based on the British Channel 4 program, *Operatunity*—followed the stories of aspiring amateur singers who were competing for a lead role in a professional opera performance of Verdi's *Rigoletto* at the Sydney Opera House.

The Choir of Hard Knocks continues this narrative strategy. Each week its viewers followed a group of socially marginalised people, as they learn how to work together as a functioning choir. Under the guidance of choir director and former Opera Australia principal Jonathan Welch, the participants acquired the technical and the personal life skills needed to reach their goal of putting on a professional public performance. As is the case with any good reality-television program, however, there are other, more profound goals, some of which reveal themselves over the life of the series—to learn how to trust others, to develop self-confidence, or to reconnect with estranged families.

However, *The Choir of Hard Knocks* represents a significant commercial and cultural advance on *Operatunity Oz* in the way in which it adapts the reality-television format originally perfected by the commercial networks. This format gives audiences numerous opportunities to participate in different ways, at different levels of creative engagement, and in various media; they might choose to view the television program, attend one or more of the choir's performances, buy the CD or DVD of the series in a store or online, read about the program or the various choir members in a magazine or newspaper article, or even join the expanding waiting list of applicants for choir membership. This sophisticated format, with its integrated marketing strategy, is familiar from a commercial television show like *Australian Idol,* in which the contestants can appear at the Sydney Opera House—as, indeed, they do for each season's finale—or at a local shopping centre or regional arts venue. *The Choir of Hard Knocks* is an example of the ABC using the reality-television format's full marketing potential to achieve public benefit.

Supporting *The Choir*—as project and as actual choir—is an extensive social network that reaches into the civic fabrics of Victoria, New South Wales and beyond. Consider some of the names involved: the ABC, Jimmy Barnes, Jonathan Welch, Melbourne City Council, the RecLink charity, Mark Trevorrow, and the Sydney Opera House. This social network spans public, private, non-profit, commercial, arts, charity and media organisations; it has the potential to continue the project—a second season is surely warranted—and further adapt it to deliver more public benefits. Participating in the project is one way for the Sydney Opera House to perform its public role in an innovative manner that builds public trust, and at the same time spreads the costs and risks of doing so.

Performing arts centres also need to cultivate trusting relationships with companies and their audiences. Opera Queensland is currently experiencing a renewed popularity among the young. The company's chief executive and artistic director, Chris Mangin, has announced that 20 per cent of its audience was under 26, up from a mere 5 per cent in 1998.[33] Mangin observes that opera audiences are growing 'as people start to recognise the quality of the vocal skills that go into it', and as the art-form becomes integrated into the lifestyles of the young: 'They're out for a really good night; they've frequently gone to dinner before or they're going clubbing after; it's all part of that entertainment mix.'[34] For performing arts centres to prosper artistically and financially they need to be able to carve a place and a role for themselves in this mix. It is important for the performing arts to be able to extend any audience's experience across limitations of geography, art-form and time, but especially so in the case of young audiences, who demand and expect it.

An audience that can move with apparent ease between opera and hip-hop, a traditional auditorium and a nightclub dance floor possesses more than 'omnivorous' cultural tastes; it is using some very different sets of social skills. Omnivorous cultural tastes are modelled and validated on a daily basis in numerous social contexts, including popular television programs. Some might find it odd to look to the power ballads of *Australian Idol* for explanations of a new appreciation of operatic vocal skills among the young. Cultural omnivores, who roam more freely across genres and art-forms, know no such inhibition.

The ABC-TV program *Spicks and Specks* is another case in point.[35] This is a panel show in which two teams compete in their knowledge of a wide variety of musical genres. Teams may include the occasional univore with a specialised knowledge of opera or country music, but for that cultural capital to be validated and for the team to win the game, the specialists need to be able to work with their team-mates. The audience can also pool its cultural capital when viewing the show in groups, and thus share both the satisfaction and social benefits of cultivating an omnivorous taste in music. This very popular television program provides all its viewers, both group and individual, with social 'water-cooler' moments for the following day. *Australian Idol* and *Spicks and Specks* are two examples of the way in which television is able to demonstrate and validate a more or less wide-ranging taste in music for a mass audience.

The young people who are making the decision to include opera attendance in their entertainment budgets expect to derive benefits that outweigh their outlay of time, effort and money. The personal and social skills and benefits they see being validated on television are factors in these deliberations. When people with young children are making decisions about the mix that is right for them, they weigh up additional factors, such as the expense and convenience of childcare. The crucial question for performing arts centres is how they can most effectively support audiences to make participation choices that are compatible with those audiences' current interests and ambitions.

6

The strength of weak ties

Like other pillar organisations, performing arts centres must respond to the needs and aspirations of diverse communities: arts professionals, committed audiences, non-attenders who may or may not value the arts, but who are conscious of their opportunity costs, tourists and strangers. These diverse demands require centres to adopt innovative programming and other management strategies that package and enhance visitors' experiences by extending those experiences over time, space and art-forms. For a performing arts venue, building trusting relationships with audiences and communities is not a short-term goal, however: it demands consistency, patience and a willingness to experiment.

In 2004 QPAC sought to build on the popularity of musicals with Brisbane audiences. In conjunction with the Queen-Ben Elton jukebox musical, *We Will Rock You*, the Centre piloted an audience development project called 'We Will Match You', addressed to potential younger audiences who may not have thought of a concert hall as a promising venue for making new acquaintances. The Centre partnered with an online-dating agency, which supplied a database of clients for the pilot. Potential participants were contacted and invited to attend a performance and social functions around that performance. The results were mixed, with the pilot attracting only a small number of participants, most of whom were not potential return visitors. Despite these results QPAC persisted, changing the name of the program to 'AdmitONE' and abandoning the dating rationale, which patrons had found to be either too confronting or unresponsive to their needs.

AdmitONE is managed by a QPAC staff member who chooses a number of performances per year, covering a range of genres. A mix of musicals, plays, operas, orchestral performances and ballets gives choices that encourage participation and returns, while providing the participants with an entrée to the QPAC repertoire that can launch them onto their own journeys of artistic discovery. The program is highly patron-driven, in that the manager responds to the stated preferences of participants. When making programming choices and seating arrangements, the manager is also guided by basic demographic and taste data provided by the participants.

For a nominal amount above the price of an A-reserve seat, participants have access to a designated ancillary space in the Centre, where they meet before the performance and during the interval. This open space, situated in the dramatically formal areas around the performance halls, adds a special ambience; AdmitONE participants feel 'spoiled'. Hosts facilitate introductions and discreetly supervise group interactions during the reception-style events. AdmitONE is not a dating service, however; it provides opportunities for single people, groups of friends or workmates, newcomers to the city, or those whose partner does not share their cultural tastes, to occupy QPAC's civic spaces and meet others in a safe and tolerant environment.

As an exercise in trust-building, AdmitONE must engage with an active constituency that has its own expectations and values. The program allows the Centre to forge productive connections between individual or private experience and civic or public values. For instance, AdmitONE patrons can develop their existing artistic tastes and knowledge while deepening and expanding their current social relationships, even as they build new social networks and identities.

South-east Queensland is the fastest-growing region in Australia and the arts are particularly well-placed to integrate new residents into its cultural, economic and civic life. AdmitONE responds to the values of potential visitors, even as it provides the infrastructure that enables them to cross cultural, geographic and social borders. It is an example of how culture can provide a safe space that encourages and supports the kinds of sociability that are so important in a complex and rapidly changing society.

Since 'trust' is a major topic in the burgeoning and influential field of 'social capital' studies, it is worth considering what researchers in the field have to say on the topic. 'Social capital' refers to the resources for collective action that are embodied in membership of social networks. Indicators of social capital include the number of neighbours one can call on in an emergency and expressions of the generalised trust that is placed in the police force or the arts, or of the more specific kind of trust that is felt for the local policeman or performing arts centre. The theoretical literature identifies two main types of social capital, bonding (involving social networks of people with similar attributes) and bridging (derived from social networks that cross demographic categories). Bridging is the most important kind for developing a community of persons with capacities and tastes for tolerance, the free exchange of knowledge and values, and the kinds of civic relationships that Mark Granovetter calls 'weak ties'.[36]

■

The social capital concept has proved to be highly adaptable; it now provides rationales and indicators for many kinds of activities and organisations requiring public or private support, from libraries and sports facilities to medical clinics and housing estates. The primary concern of much of the early social capital research was with improving the delivery of welfare services, or the social and economic integration of the unemployed[37] or of otherwise marginalised people.[38] Other researchers have used the concept to understand how arts participation can be a remedy for social exclusion and disadvantage.[39] The participatory arts, with their 'instrumental' rationales and traditional disregard for aesthetic values, have seemed a natural fit for research into the ways in which the arts generate social capital.[40] More recent research applies the concept to the role played by performing arts organisations in building and maintaining cultural vitality and resilient communities: in other words, social capital as a way of understanding how culture and the arts can contribute to community capacity-building.[41]

Since the 1990s, the World Bank has popularised a definition of social capital as 'the glue that binds'.[42] A problem with this functionalist definition—as well as with the development path it sets out to build—is that it does not account for forms of social capital that do not bind a whole community around a common goal of working towards greater stability and prosperity. While organised crime groups do not trust outsiders, they have strong internal ties. Cultural univores who identify closely with their consumption are likely to form closed social networks and engage in 'turf wars' with other groups over issues like the allocation of rehearsal time, or relative levels of public funding for 'their' art-form. In the arts, as elsewhere, more social capital is not necessarily a good thing. Also, different kinds of trust—such as trust in family, neighbours and government—have different causes and effects. These differences have to be acknowledged when subjective levels of 'trust' are used as indicators of social capital.[43]

The functionalist account of social capital has particular limitations when applied to participation in culture and the arts. Since it takes compulsory participation as its ideal, it doesn't acknowledge that people have a right not to participate, nor that, when they do, it is perfectly legitimate for them to be transported by the power of art without expecting a social payoff. The former problem is political, while the latter is a failure to accommodate non-instrumental values.

Performing arts centres are often criticised for not creating and sustaining open social networks: it is said that they are unable to bridge social groups and, instead, foster mono-cultural enclaves that emphasise bonding. In short, the centres have been seen as elitist and as working against inclusive civic goals, as distinct from financial or aesthetic ones. While centre administrators do face real problems in broadening participation and diversifying programming, the social capital concept provides reasons for qualifying this received wisdom.

Performing arts centres use free pre-show talks to increase audiences' understanding and appreciation of some of their productions. In 2004, we partnered with QPAC to conduct a series of focus groups involving people who had seen a variety of QPAC productions. Focus-group members who had attended these talks reported that it made them feel special: they were getting insights other people weren't getting; they felt they were part of an exclusive club. A sense of bonding can be a powerful inducement to attend and has an obvious role to play in achieving the financial goals of an organisation. Since the sense of bonding derived from shared routines, pleasures, knowledge and skills adds value to an audiences' aesthetic experience, it has proved useful for audience development programs. Aesthetic and economic values do intersect here.

Participation in the pre-show talks was not only a bonding exercise, however; it built audience members' capacities and inclinations to engage with strangers. Some people reported that these new social bonds were extended beyond the talk and performance: groups met later for a drink and conversation about their experiences, and people spoke of how these experiences influenced their relationships with fellow audience members, how they came to value others perspectives, and how they learnt to reflect on their own tastes and experiences. In this case, bonding acted as a potential 'sweetener' for bridging experiences during and after the performance, bridging experiences that foster 'weak ties' that have civic benefits. Admittedly, it can be difficult to identify those benefits, to track the spillovers from talking to strangers. It is hard to quantify this ineffability, this refusal to be pinned down and owned that is the essence of a public good.

7

Partnerships and cultural exchange

Strategic partnerships enable performing arts centres to create public value by linking into local, national and international professional networks and cultural exchanges. The performing arts have long been leaders in promoting international exchange and co-operation as performers and companies have worked an international circuit. Actors, dancers and opera singers have long sought and achieved international fame, not just by having travellers come to their performances, but by themselves touring and making recordings. Similarly, the capacity of performing arts centres to host touring companies and showcase local talent in the same venue has long been valued, both for its ability to raise local standards and as a powerful expression of civic pride and prestige. This capacity is becoming more important now that service provision is being emphasised over goods production, and the speed and volume of global flows of people, goods and services is rapidly increasing.

Previously, the arts had a role in a civic space dominated by knowledge silos and arts 'factories'. Today, as Thomas Friedman notes,

> 'what' you make is quickly copied and sold by everyone, but 'how' you engage your customers,

> 'how' you keep your promises, and 'how' you collaborate with partners—that's not so easy to copy, and that is where companies can really differentiate themselves.[44]

The reference is to generic firms, yet the point is no less relevant to arts organisations looking to add value to public life by partnering with government, business and communities. These partnerships are configuring new civic spaces in which social networks, trust-building and a focus on service provision are the keys to successful public-value outcomes.

Public/private partnerships are currently being promoted by governments keen to share the cost of the provision of public goods and services. But public/public partnerships also have an important role to play in extending the reach of arts organisations. Cultural institutions have common interests in attracting resources, expanding markets and raising their public profile. Partnerships with national broadcasters are also well-established. While federal responsibility for the arts has long been linked with communications (which also gets the lion's share of federal funding), at state level the arts portfolio has been mobile, and variously attached to tourism, sport, heritage, the environment and education. It is rare to find arts and culture as stand-alone departments, or as part of a premier's department, though premiers have occasionally been known to take an interest in various ways.

Current interest in the well-being of children and young people, coupled with an expectation that arts organisations will expand young audiences, has highlighted the importance of strategic partnerships with state education departments, and with academics who have expertise in early childhood. These partnerships enable exchanges of expertise and build capacity on both sides. The Adelaide Festival Centre, for example, developed its CentreED education program in consultation with the South Australian Department of Education and Children's Services. CentreED provides department-accredited professional development opportunities for teachers. The AFC also hosts workshops and courses for teachers and students under its *SACE Drama Day* and *SACE Dance Day* programs. These day-long performances and workshops enable year-12 drama students and teachers to work with industry professionals. The Centre also works with the Education Department, the *Come Out* children's arts festival and Ausdance, to run workshops for primary-school students. These workshops integrate visual and performing arts experiences and introduce the children to the Festival Centre, which is Adelaide's principal professional dance space. In addition to these regularly scheduled events, CentreED provides one-off professional training opportunities in conjunction with arts companies like Flying Penguin Productions.

Public benefits accrue from such partnerships: they help participating organisations with a brief to add public value to the performing arts to better co-ordinate their policies and programs; they build teaching and artistic capacities; they expose students at all levels of education to industry role models in professional working contexts; and they forge bonds of mutual understanding and trust between participants, between the participants and the partnering organisations, and among the partners themselves.

In addition to partnering with state education departments, performing arts centres create public value by working with local community groups, publicly-funded representative organisations, and the corporate sector. QPAC, for instance, runs the highly successful *Out of the Box* festival for young children and their parents or other adult guardians. By working with state and local government and the corporate sector, QPAC has been able to build *Out of the Box* into an exportable format that enhances the Centre's international profile and prestige. In 2007 QPAC also partnered with the Brisbane City Council, the South Bank Corporation, corporate sponsors and federal government agencies to host the inaugural *Bonyi International Music Festival*, during which school-age musicians and singers from Australia, New Zealand and South Africa performed and attended workshops with international teachers. In addition, QPAC hosts events for children during the annual *Buddha Birthday Festival* held in the adjoining South Bank cultural precinct.

Partnerships between performing arts centres and ethnic community groups can help unlock the resources of Australia's culturally diverse population. They are especially useful for building social capital at a local level, as well as for integrating the centres and their communities into international cultural exchanges. These working relationships ensure that 'multicultural programming' is more than the representation of other peoples and their cultures. When there are no partnerships that give the represented a say, or when existing ones lack true reciprocity, cultural exchange is reduced to the so-called 'cultural veneers' of food stalls or art-and-craft displays. These popular forms of participation are placed in a broader perspective when cultural exchanges are understood in terms of the relationships of mutual trust and understanding they entail, and the public value flowing from those relationships.

In recent years Adelaide has seen a significant increase in new arrivals from various African cultural groups. Faced with this demographic change and greater cultural diversity, and conscious of its mandate to provide cultural leadership, the AFC has developed new partnerships with the African Communities Council of South Australia (ACCSA) and the Migrant Resource Centre of South Australia (MRCSA). The Festival Centre's aim in establishing these relationships was to encourage and facilitate participation by African communities in a Pan-African Festival. This festival was held for the first time in 2006. While it featured a variety of music and dance performances, as well as food, art-and-craft stalls, its main goals and enduring civil significance concerned the 'how'. Joseph Masika of the ACCSA described the mixed motivations and expectations of his organisation and the communities in the following terms:

> We wish to hold our Pan-African Festival at the Adelaide Festival Centre because we wish to showcase our diverse cultures for our own communities and for the wider multicultural Australian community. Most importantly we want to demonstrate that we are the 'united African communities of South Australia'. Your Centre is secure and self-contained and in the centre of the city, close to public transport, crucial to our people. The Centre gives us a

> professional venue with a high public profile and we share your goals of free and cultural expression.[45]

The AFC used its strategic partnerships to produce a range of public-value benefits: ethnic cultural affiliations that are open and 'weak', in the sense of being articulated in relation to a shared identification with Australia; increased levels of cross-cultural understanding for individuals and communities; mutual trust-building between African immigrant communities and a prestigious institution that plays a key role in the cultural and civil life of the state; and a public confirmation that these recently-arrived people are valued members of the greater community. These public-value outcomes are produced by a new civil space formed by the partnerships.

The public value of cultural exchange is not always appreciated. In a recent report for the Demos think-tank in the UK, Kirsten Bound and colleagues note that, while leaders and countries have always used culture to confirm their identities, assert power and build relationships, the worth of cultural diplomacy is typically overshadowed by that of the 'harder stuff', such as military capability, international laws and treaties. When such channels are absent, under-developed or too rigid to ensure effective communication, cultural exchange still 'gives us the chance to appreciate points of commonality and, where there are differences, to understand the motivations and humanity that underlie them'.[46]

It is culture's ability to forge resilient social relationships below the levels of national or state governments that gives it an advantage over public diplomacy. Culture need not be a tool of public diplomacy to have public value; in fact, its 'soft power' is actually derived from its distance from political direction. Today's high-stake encounters between the local and the global pose serious dangers, as well as offer great rewards. Many of the pressing problems we now face—from climate change to terrorism and the management of immigration—do not respond to the old 'hard power' solutions. In the contemporary world, the 'soft power' of cultural exchanges has a new importance.[47]

The experience of performing arts centres in brokering cultural exchanges can help them contribute to cultural diplomacy. The way the centres operate at arm's length from governments enhances their credibility and flexibility. They have expertise in working with international artists and companies, as well as in finding and developing local audiences for the new and unfamiliar. They provide safe spaces where audiences, artists, technicians and administrators from different cultural groups can meet, share their cultural wares, skills and stories and learn from those exchanges. Centre-based lighting crews work with visiting Chinese contemporary dance companies; South American singers collaborate with local musicians; sets can be designed and built in Adelaide in consultation with Asian artists and clients and exported throughout the region, thus developing social networks and further opportunities for cultural exchanges. The centres' capacities for leadership in cultural diplomacy can serve them well in delivering public-value outcomes, not only for local individuals and communities, or for Australians as a whole, but for people in other parts of the world who likewise benefit from the resilient relationships produced by cultural exchange.

8

A bold cultural statement

The public conversation about Sydney and Melbourne's status as 'world cities' has continued. In her address of welcome to the Sydney Writers' Festival, Sydney Lord Mayor Clover Moore assured the audience that creative thinkers and cultural organisations would be involved in consultations about the City Council's strategic plan for a 'sustainable Sydney'. Former CEO at the Opera House, and latterly CEO at London's Southbank Centre, Michael Lynch has put arts and culture at the centre of his bid to be elected Lord Mayor of Sydney. *SMH* columnists have continued to provoke, on subjects including style and public architecture.

Meantime in Melbourne, a conversation is unfolding around the topic 'Future Melbourne' at a series of forums sponsored by the City Council and held at Melbourne University. At one of these public forums, which aim to explore 'key urban issues', including cultural identity, historian Clare Wright said recently:

> Melbourne has never been a showy place—even its Commonwealth Games spectacle used a duck rather than sequins to focus the world's attention. [...] Melbourne is a serious place. Much as Manhattan has made anxiety and neurosis a centrepiece of its

> cultural attraction, Melbourne has proudly worn its head on its sleeve.[48]

In addition to these events, citizens can share views at the 'Future Melbourne' website's evillage, an electronic town meeting, the agenda of which is organised around eleven 'talking points', including knowledge and culture. Participants are invited to

> [j]oin the *Talk Culture* online community and discuss, debate and share [their] ideas on the culture and identity of Melbourne and how these might evolve including: what [they] love about the city and its people; what makes something or someone 'Melburnian'; [Melbourne's] rich cultural diversity; the role of the arts as an expression of this culture; culture for people all ages and abilities; public art; major events and festivals; indigenous arts; arts grant programs; heritage and history; arts investment; and arts participation.[49]

So how can those who see themselves as part of the arts community—artists and performers, patrons and audiences, administrators, educators and critics, and the wider public—engage in this emergent public sphere?

The web offers opportunities to go beyond transactions to interactions, to build relationships and to create a new cultural vernacular. The new cultural leadership requires a subtle understanding of the nature of demand in a world of connectivity. For arts organisations, this means more than marketing, more than providing information about events and programs, more than online ticket purchase. In the UK, the funding available through the National Lottery has been used to support culture online. The National Theatre's Stagework site is one outcome of this project. In the US, the Brooklyn Museum is inviting the public to become 'friends' through its Myspace, Facebook, and Flickr sites.[50] 'Friends' are posting comments, and photographs of themselves and the exhibits. Over time, the museum will gather a fascinating pictorial record of the way the public values its museum. A genuinely engaging public conversation about the importance of the arts and culture will reveal how the public values culture, not just in the here-and-now but for the future.

It is a big challenge, but as creativity is more widely dispersed, the demand for more arts experiences will grow. Psychologist Mihaly Csikszentmihalyi's influential theory of 'flow' sets out to explain how creativity enriches lives at the level of the individual.[51] But a key question he raises concerns not the 'who', but the 'where', of creativity. Innovation in the symbolic domain, whether in the arts or sciences, occurs when curiosity and discovery, driven by a creative individual, *changes established practice* in a given domain. Practice changes only when the potential of an innovation is recognised and supported by the brokers of knowledge within a particular domain. But widespread adoption of innovation depends on the field's connection to the wider social system. In the arts, this points to the importance of patronage in all its guises. And that will—must—involve all of us.

Endnotes

1 *Sydney Morning Herald (SMH),* 5-6 May 2007, p. 42.
2 'Art's great hope left hanging', *SMH,* 5-6 May 2007, p. 37.
3 *The Rise of the Creative Class* (North Melbourne: Pluto Press, 2003).
4 Quoted by Saul Eslake, 'Economists and the arts', *Artshub,* 24 April 2007, available at http://www.artshub.com.au/au/news.asp?sId=157239# (accessed 30 April 2007).
5 Chris Anderson, *The Long Tail: Why the Future of Business Is Selling Less of More* (London: Random House, 2006).
6 François Matarasso, *Defining Values: Evaluating Arts Programmes,* Social Impact of the Arts Working Paper 1 (Stroud, UK: Comedia, 1996), p. 5.
7 Robert H. McNulty, Dorothy R. Jacobson and R. Leo Penne, *The Economics of Amenity: Community Futures and Quality of Life: A Policy Guide to Urban Economic Development* (Washington, DC: Partners for Livable Communities, 1985), p. 49.
8 Danny Quah, quoted by Diane Coyle, *The Weightless World: Strategies for Managing the Digital Economy* (Cambridge, Mass.: MIT Press, 1999), p. 3.
9 *The Rise of the Creative Class* [Review], *Platform,* 5.2 (October 2006), p. 11.
10 Quoted in *The Weightless World,* p. 22.

11 'Social computing priorities', *Australian,* 3 July 2007, IT Business, p. 1.
12 Available at http://actsofcreation.theartscentre.net.au (accessed 27 June 2007).
13 (London: Vintage, 2006), pp. 171-2.
14 *Saturday,* p. 68.
15 Michael Goldhaber [Blog], available at < http://www.goldhaber.org/> (accessed 27 July 2007).
16 'The Economics of Attention', Edge Perspectives with John Hagel, available at http://edgeperspectives.typepad.com (accessed 29 June 2007).
17 *Distinction: A Social Critique of the Judgement of Taste* (London: RKP, 1986).
18 Richard Peterson and M. Kern, 'Changing highbrow taste: from snob to omnivore', *American Sociological Review,* 61.5 (1996), pp. 900-07.
19 *Distinction,* p. 12.
20 Kevin F. McCarthy and others, *Gifts of the Muse: Reframing the Debate about the Benefits of the Arts* (Santa Monica, Calif.: RAND Corporation, 2005).
21 *The Values Study: Rediscovering the Meaning and Value of Arts Participation* (Hartford: Connecticut Commission on Culture and Tourism, 2004).
22 'An Architecture of Public Value', *Grantmakers in the Arts Reader,* 17.1 (Spring 2006), pp. 18-25.
23 Available at http://www.stagework.org/webdav/harmonise?Page/@id=6000 (accessed 9 June 2007).
24 John Holden, *Logging On: Culture, Participation and the Web* (London: Demos, 2007), p. 19, available at www.demos.co.uk (accessed 3 June 2007).
25 *Boundaries and Allegiances,* p. 113.
26 *Talking Heads,* ABC-TV series, Brisbane, Producer Nick Lee (2005).
27 Kevin Harris and Martin Dudley, *Public Libraries and Community Cohesion: Developing Indicators*

(London: Museums, Libraries & Archives Council, 2005), p. 11.

28 Harris and Dudley, p. 7.

29 Glenn D. Lowry, 'A Deontological Approach to Art Museums and the Public Trust', in *Whose Muse?: Art Museums and the Public Trust*, ed. by James Cuno (Princeton, NJ: Princeton University Press, 2004) pp. 133-4.

30 *Ibid.*

31 *The Choir of Hard Knocks,* ABC-TV series, Melbourne, Executive Producer Alison Black (2007).

32 *Operatunity Oz,* ABC-TV series, Producer Nick Lee (2006).

33 Anooska Tucker-Evans, 'Opera is cool for the young crowd', *Courier-Mail,* 13 May 2007, p. 23.

34 *Ibid.*

35 *Spicks and Specks,* ABC-TV series, Sydney, Producer Anthony Watt (2006).

36 'The Strength of Weak Ties', *American Journal of Sociology*, 81 (1973), pp. 1287-303.

37 David Gyarmati and Darrell Kyte, 'Social Capital, Network Formation and the Community Employment Innovation Project', *Horizons: Policy Research Initiative,* 6: 3 (2003), available at http://policyresearch.gc.ca/page.asp?pagenm=v6n3_art_05 (accessed 20 July 2007).

38 Jean Tillie, 'Social Capital and the Political Integration of Immigrants,' *International Conference on the Opportunity and Challenge of Diversity: A Role for Social Capital?* (2003), available at http://policyresearch.gc.ca/page.asp?pagenm=OECD_Background#session5 (accessed 6 April 2007).

39 Deborah Mills and Paul Brown, *Art and Wellbeing* (Surry Hills, NSW: Australia Council for the Arts, 2004).

40 See Deidre Williams, *Creating Social Capital: A Study of the Long-term Benefits from Community-Based Arts Funding* (Adelaide: Community Arts Network of South Australia, 1995) and also Matarasso, *Defining Values* (1996).

41 Kay Ferres and David Adair, 'Social Capital, Communities and Recent Rationales for the Performing Arts'. International Conference on Engaging Communities, 14-17 August 2005 in Brisbane (Brisbane: UNESCO / Queensland Government), available at http://www.engagingcommunities2005.org/abstracts/Ferres-Kay-final.pdf, (accessed 2 July 2007).

42 Edward W. Bresnyan Jr., Maria Alejandra Bouquet & Francesca Russo, *MBOPs and the Case of Northeast Brazil: The Rural Poverty Reduction Program* (Washington, DC: World Bank, 2003).

43 Toby Fattore, Nick Turnbull and Shaun Wilson, '"More Community!": Does the Social Capital Hypothesis Offer Hope for Untrusting Societies', *The Drawing Board: An Australian Review of Public Affairs,* 3.3 (March 2003), p. 168. See also *Creating Social Trust in Post-Socialist Transitions*, ed. by Bo Rothstein, János Kornai and Susan Rose-Ackerman (London: Palgrave Macmillan, 2004).

44 'Ever-watchful little brother makes for good citizens and businesses', *Sydney Morning Herald,* 29 June 2007, p. 13.

45 Quoted in *Annual Report, 2005-06* (Adelaide: Adelaide Festival Centre, 2006), p. 35.

46 Kirsten Bound and others, *Cultural Diplomacy* (London: Demos, 2007), p. 11.

47 Bound and others, pp. 12-13.

48 'The city that wears its head on its sleeve', *Age*, 14 June 2007, p. 17.

49 'Future Melbourne', available at www.futuremelbourne.

com.au (accessed 1 July 2007).

50 'Brooklyn Museum', available at http://www.brooklynmuseum.org/community/network (accessed 9 July 2007).

51 *Creativity: Flow and the Psychology of Discovery and Invention* (New York: HarperCollins, 1996).

Readers' Forum

Responses to Lee Lewis' *Cross-racial Casting: Changing the Face of Australian Theatre*

Teik-Kim Pok, an Honours graduate in Theatre and founder member of the contemporary performance group, Shagging Julie, is obsessed with issues of cross-cultural hybridity. Last August he was one of twenty-four international artists chosen to explore the crossing of imaginary cultural and political borders at a workshop run by Guillermo Gómez-Peña's La Pocha Nostra performance group in Tucson.

As a male, Chinese, Malaysian-born, Singapore-bred and recently-naturalized Australian actor-performer based in Sydney, I have only had limited experience of being rejected on the basis of skin colour or cultural background—mainly because I work on the independent or 'contemporary performance' scene.

We might discuss social and cultural taboos that we challenge in our work, but my fellow-performers and I rarely ask whether our audiences take in the Western (Anglo) classical repertoire as part of their cultural diet. That's not to say that new, devised work is entirely innocent of what social commentator Boris Frankel calls 'cultural enclosure' of the myopic, Lilliputian kind, an attitude that's applicable to the main-stage casting practice that Lee Lewis describes as the 'filofax phenomenon' (p. 20).

I've had both positive and negative experiences. At university here in Sydney I was cast in a variety of roles from both the classical and modern Anglo repertoire. Once—I had a substantial supporting role in Shakespeare's *Tempest*—I took it as a back-handed compliment that audience members were surprised that an Oriental male could speak the iambic pentameter without stumbling! On another occasion, playing the five-line cameo of the butler in Tom Stoppard's *Arcadia*, I was saddened to overhear a fellow actor loudly cast doubt on the likelihood of finding Chinese butlers in the country houses of nineteenth-century England! Instead of coming back with a witty 'But they'd heard about Melbourne and had come to Derbyshire to pan for gold', or showing him the blind alley up which the legacy of nineteenth-century naturalism had led us, I decided that propping up Dead/Decrepit White Male literary traditions was not a long-term career path for me.

I could see my Chinese elders wagging their fingers at me for wanting a life in the performing arts and raising a collective raised eyebrow in the self-satisfied fashion of 'I told you so'. Nonetheless, I was not alone and, thanks to the support of organizations such as Performance Space, PACT and Urban Theatre Projects, soon found myself devising new and hybrid work with collaborators of countless cultural and various art-form backgrounds. And it was a huge relief to no longer have to face the humiliating experience of the audition and inevitable rejection that followed: 'Sorry, not really suitable!'

Today, eight years later, I am in Tucson, Arizona, part of a training workshop run by Guillermo Gómez-Peña and La Pocha Nostra, his San Francisco-based performance group, and hoping to learn how we might make this hybrid-casting business work for Australia's main stages. The manifesto of La Pocha Nostra asserts, in part, that 'if we learn to cross borders on stage, we may learn how to do so in larger social spheres'. A central aim of the workshop, which involves twenty-four other artists from around the globe, is to discover 'new ways of relating to our own bodies'. We must first, writes Gómez-Peña, 'de-colonize them, then repoliticize them as sites for pleasure and penance, for memory and reinvention, for action and refraction' (*ethno-techno: Writings on performance, activism and pedagogy* (Routledge, 2005), p.98). This is to be achieved, in the next ten days, by participants from across a wide spectrum of art forms (directors, performers, musicians, visual and digital artists etc) and ethnic origins (Okinanwan, Anglo-Vietnamese, Mexican, Cuban, Scottish, Columbian, Chinese-Malaysian and, of course, Australian), undertaking a regime of repeated and cumulative exercises in non-verbal communication and co-creation. The inspiration for Gómez-Peña's methodology derives from pedagogy that seeks to develop 'new models for relationships between artists and communities, mentor and apprentice, which are neither colonial nor condescending' (*ethno-techno*, p. 98), a long-term project that we, as a community of self-appointed questioners of the status quo, should seek to apply to all our art-forms, not just the theatre. To repudiate this and assume that audiences will be uncomfortable with mixed-race casts—or any 'radical' element, for that matter—in main-stage classical work is arrogant and patronising, and underestimates an audience's wish / ability to engage with what that profound ritual, the Theatre of the Human Condition.

As a so-called avant-garde, hybridity-favouring and coloured performer-devisor, I confess to having some of these elitist leanings. I am, however, ready to move forward—not only by voicing loud support for Lee Lewis's exhortation to embrace cross-ethnic casting in classical work, but also by urging us, in all of our creative processes, to do more than pay lip-service to the idea of Genuine Dialogue. We cannot afford to revert to the Parochial Monologue. The ultimate price that we will pay for that is the deadening of the very source of our inspiration as artists, an ability to at once observe and celebrate diversity and unity.

Diana Simmonds is a founder member of the Sydney Theatre Reviewers group, editor of www.stagenoise.com and a Wog.

'Changing the face of Australian theatre' *is* something that probably is happening. But, tectonic plates being what they are, Lee Lewis's intervention is to be welcomed. However, to achieve anything beyond disgruntled hissing in dark corners, interventions need to be better thought out than the scattergun approach adopted in *Platform Papers No.13*.

First, there is the vexed question of what to call these wretched actors of a tinted or semi-tinted persuasion who are not content with playing maids, morons, tarts and crims. Lewis says: 'I shall follow Ghassan Hage's lead and be provocative, rather than uncomfortable.' Que? TWLP? It's certainly provocative. I mean, who wants to approximate a rare frog farting in a small pond in Arnhem Land? As for NESB ... having homogeneity thrust upon one is as bad for the morale as having Whiteness held up as the ideal.

'Third-World-Looking People' is ridiculous and insulting, while 'Non-English Speaking Background' could apply to as many semi-literate, ill-educated 'Australians' as it does to those of us who arrived by public transport rather than the birth canal. The need for non-invasive labelling goes with the earnest social services mentality revealed in Lewis's ambition of developing 'Australian hybrid work' (place in the bins provided when flying interstate) which will 'incorporate progressive targets for actor training, writer development, geographically specific audience consultation, directorial and management re-education and programming'. Meanwhile, let's march around the parade ground, chanting 'Two acts good, one act better'. Then rally down at the Wharf to demand KPIs for all artistic directors and RDOs for all actors. No, sorry: most actors already *are* on semi-permanent RDOs.

It's not that I don't think Lewis is on to something really important in looking at the overwhelming Whiteness of the Australian stage and wondering why. And what can and should be done about it? It's not just theatre, though. She illustrates the overwhelming nature of the problem in noting that Hollywood has a tradition of assimilating actors of differently-abled origins by Whitening their names—Ramon Estevez/Martin Sheen, Ilyena Mironovna/Helen Mirren, Alphonso D'Abruzzo/Alan Alda etc.

Cross-cultural casting has been happening for decades in the entertainment industries of the UK and USA. And the leaders, ironically, are in TV. Think *Hill Street Blues*, which made its debut in 1981. In the twenty-first century, it's still cop shows, including the derided but multi-hued *The Bill*, and hospital dramas (*ER*, *Gray's Anatomy* et al) that cast across cultures. Unless they're Australian handcuff-and-bandage shows, of course, then the only certainty in casting is Georgie Parker.

And the divine Parker is actually a good example: she's White, but could be cast as Italian, Greek, South American, Cypriot, Russian, Indian or—insert exotic here—and nobody (aside from rejected Wogs) would blink. Turn it around and ask how often, let's say, Gia and Zoe Carides or Dina Panozzo are cast as other than sultry Latin temptresses? Further irony: when Panozzo scored a rare continuing TV role where ethnicity wasn't an issue, in Ten's *Richmond Hill,* she played a real-estate agent—not among the most admired occupations.

Nevertheless, to cast these performers with regard only to their perceived ethnicity is to insult them in several ways – which Australian casting directors and directors seem only too happy to do. It is impossible to imagine a cast as ethnically and culturally diverse as that of *The Bill* or *Gray's Anatomy* on Australian television. You have to wonder, therefore, at the continuing popularity in the UK of *Neighbours* and *Home and Away.* Do British audiences view them with nostalgic longing for the England of the 1950s when blacks were lavatory cleaners and garlic-munching continentals stayed on their side of the Channel?

Cross-cultural casting on our theatre stages is just one hill to climb out of the valley of the shadow of White Australia. Just as steep is the hill of scripts originating from Broadway and the West End which occupy so much time and talent in our theatres. It's not simply writer development that's needed, but writers from diverse backgrounds. Lewis cites *Anna in the Tropics* as a non-White play seen in Sydney in 2007. Yet Nilo Cruz's Pulitzer Prize winner had languished in the major companies' too-hard basket since 2003 because of its Cuban-American characters. Yet Lewis seems to think casting actors of mainly Greek and Italian descent was almost as problematic as casting Georgie Parker might have been. This is hard to take and citing the colour-blindness of opera is not useful. Opera is about music, not appearance. High priest Calaf can be sung by Korean tenor Dongwong Shin, Chinese Ding Yi or white Aussie Julian Gavin; and princess Turandot by Texan soprano Jennifer Wilson, African-American Leona Mitchell or

Dame Joan Sutherland: it's the voice, not the appearance, that matters in opera.

Another so far unmentioned obstacle is class: Rebel Wilson's *The Westies Monologues* was a rare contemporary assault on overwhelmingly middle-class Australian theatre; while the *Wogs out of Work* franchise crossed class and culture. Meanwhile, however, the class hatred of overwhelmingly White *Kath and Kim* is a ratings winner. These factors will matter more and more as Australian society fractures further into richer and poorer and the traditional class structure is joined by another layer: the ethnic and economic under-class.

Australia is not as White as it was twenty years ago when I stepped off the plane, but it's still lazily, complacently and amazingly out of step with the USA and Britain in terms of cultural and ethnic inclusiveness and class awareness. And that's not saying much: these two great cultural imperialists are only about two metres ahead. But in tectonic plate terms, that could be generations.

From John Golder, editor

In *PP13*, Lee Lewis refers to a recent controversy at the Comédie-Française. In her production of the late Bernard-Marie Koltès's *Le Retour au desert*, director Muriel Mayette cast a French actor in the role of Aziz, an Algerian servant. The production opened on 17 February. Several weeks later, Bernard-Marie's brother François, the playwright's legal heir and executor, claimed that Mme Mayette had broken the terms of their contract and infringed the dramatist's moral rights. On 22 March he demanded that the play be taken off after 30 performances, and its scheduled run cut short. Mme Mayette (who is administrator-general of the theatre) reluctantly agreed, but promptly sued him for damages, looking to recover revenue lost by the cancellation of four performances in the 2006-07 season and the planned 2007-08 revival.

On 24 March, a public forum was held at the Théâtre du Vieux Colombier and a number of important issues were debated: the extent of the theatre's responsibilities towards ethnic and visible minorities; the extent of a director's rights in the work of both living and dead authors; the extent of an executor's rights over a production etc.

In an interview published in *Le Monde* on 25 March 2007, Muriel Mayette made her position very clear:

> In December [2006], [François Koltès] indicated that he realized that Michel Favory had been cast as Aziz and that he didn't like it. However, he didn't ask me to change the casting. Even if he had, I couldn't have agreed. [...] The Comédie-Française company is sufficiently cross-bred; there's a Pole, and Iranian, an Armenian, two Belgians, an African and others ... As for the author's stage directions, it says 'Aziz' and that's all. Since Koltès calls one character a 'great black paratrooper', I asked Bakary Sangaré to play the role because I wanted to follow the author's wishes as closely as I could. But, as for the two Algerians, Koltès doesn't say who should play them. For one I chose a Kosovan; though there's nothing Algerian about him. That didn't seem to worry François Koltès. And for Aziz I chose Michel Favory, whose mother is actually a Kabyle. So I reckon I have respected the wishes of the author.
>
> There have been a number of actors in the company who are Algerian by birth. [...] But to employ an Algerian to play an Algerian would show an

> alarming lack of both openness of mind and serious consideration of what theatre's all about. I do in fact believe that too few immigrant francophone actors are employed in France. But taking on an Algerian to play an Algerian is hardly the first step in that direction. It is by acknowledging and employing foreign-born actors to take on any role in the repertory. The day when not only Othello but Iago as well are played by black actors, then we shall have moved forward.

The career of Bakary Sangaré is very much to the point here. He is a west African actor, from Mali, who played Ariel in Peter Brook's French production of Shakespeare's *Tempest* in 1990, alongside the black African Sotigui Kouyaté (Prospero), the Indian Shantala Malhar-Shivalingappa (Miranda), Japanese Yoshi Oida (Gonzalo) and white Frenchman Alain Maratrat and white Englishman Bruce Myers (Stephano and Trinculo). Brook has accustomed Parisian audiences to multi-racial casting at his Bouffes du Nord theatre since the early 1970s. Recently, Sangaré has played the 'white' roles of Antoine Vitez, former administrator of the Comédie-Française, and, last season, Orgon in Molière's *Tartuffe*—both at the Comédie-Française.

Some weeks later, on 10 May, Denis Podalydès, a member of the Comédie-Française company, responded passionately in *L'Express*.

> All theatre is convention. You never see the sea there, nor the sky, you never see things as they really are [...] The greater, the more universal, the more classical the work, the more it admits of this freedom, for the work itself will live on, will always be there...
>
> François Koltès [...] doesn't understand the theatre and denies it this capacity; he reduces it, destroys it; he might have the power of the law, but not of the

> imagination. Behaving as he does, he insults, ridicules, wounds and seriously humiliates Michel Favory.[...] But each time he walks on stage as Aziz, he demonstrates brilliantly just how stupid and laughable the position adopted by François Koltès is. An actor does something very specific: he conjures into being something that doesn't exist. A man enters a room: we're told it's Hamlet, or Aziz; if his acting is good, we grant him this, he becomes that character. But you have to see him to believe this. [...] Has François Koltès actually seen Favory play Aziz? Has he seen him in the scene in Saifi's café? [...] If he were to see just this one scene, how could he persist in his pernicious, absurd, scandalous argument? [...] Is he aware that the entire Comédie-Française company, who stand with our colleague, believe that we have been wounded and insulted as much as he has?

Georges Lavaudant, outgoing director of the Odéon-Théâtre de l'Europe, agreed with Podalydès about 'the actor's capacity to play anything', but, writing in *Le Monde* on 3 June, asked that 'We respect Koltès's wishes':

> Bernard-Marie Koltès wanted a Black or an Arab on stage in every one of his plays. He systematically created roles with this in mind. We can ignore this wish, but we can't pretend it didn't exist. [...] We think that, because France is converting to multiculturalism, Koltès's kind of polemic no longer has a place. I must say that I don't share this view. Koltès wanted to make changes to our theatre. The main one concerns this question of skin-colour. He feels real anger at those reasons which permit us stage directors to refuse to do what he says and wants. He's alarmed by the crazy

> arguments we come up with to oppose him. He's indignant at our arrogance and off-handedness.
>
> Koltès understood his plays and knew what he wanted when he wrote his stage directions. His solitary, magnificent, vain fight can't be ignored or contradicted without solid arguments. He was a young man in a hurry, and set his own rules. He didn't want to wait for quotas or positive discrimination. He created his characters and demanded that they be played as he had imagined them. [...] I'm far from convinced that altering or confusing his brave message in the name of artistic freedom represents either a political or artistic solution for the future.

On 20 June the court found in favour of the theatre: François Koltès had 'failed to honour his contractual obligations and had clearly abused his moral rights'. In the European Union inherited moral rights permit a legal heir to stop a production going ahead if they believe a play's integrity has been violated and the author's wishes not respected. The judges acknowledged that Bernard-Marie Koltès had been anxious to use ethnic-minority actors, that he had complained of the extraordinary powers of directors and that he had protested whenever, in productions of his plays, Africans were not played by Africans. Nonetheless, in this instance, despite the fact that the character's name is Aziz and he speaks both French and Arabic, they concluded that 'there was nothing in the text of *Le Retour au désert* to say that Aziz must be played by an Arab or an Algerian'. Nor did they acknowledge Koltès's clear intentions, constantly enunciated during his lifetime: 'You can no more act a race than a gender.'

François Koltès was ordered to pay the Comédie-Française 20,000 Euros in damages—the theatre had originally sought 200,000 Euros—plus a further 10,000 Euros in court costs. He lodged an appeal. Also on 20 June, in a neighbouring courtroom, another judge was hearing a separate charge of defamation, brought by the Comédie: Koltès had reportedly called Mme Mayette 'cynical'. Final judgments are to be handed down on 12 September.

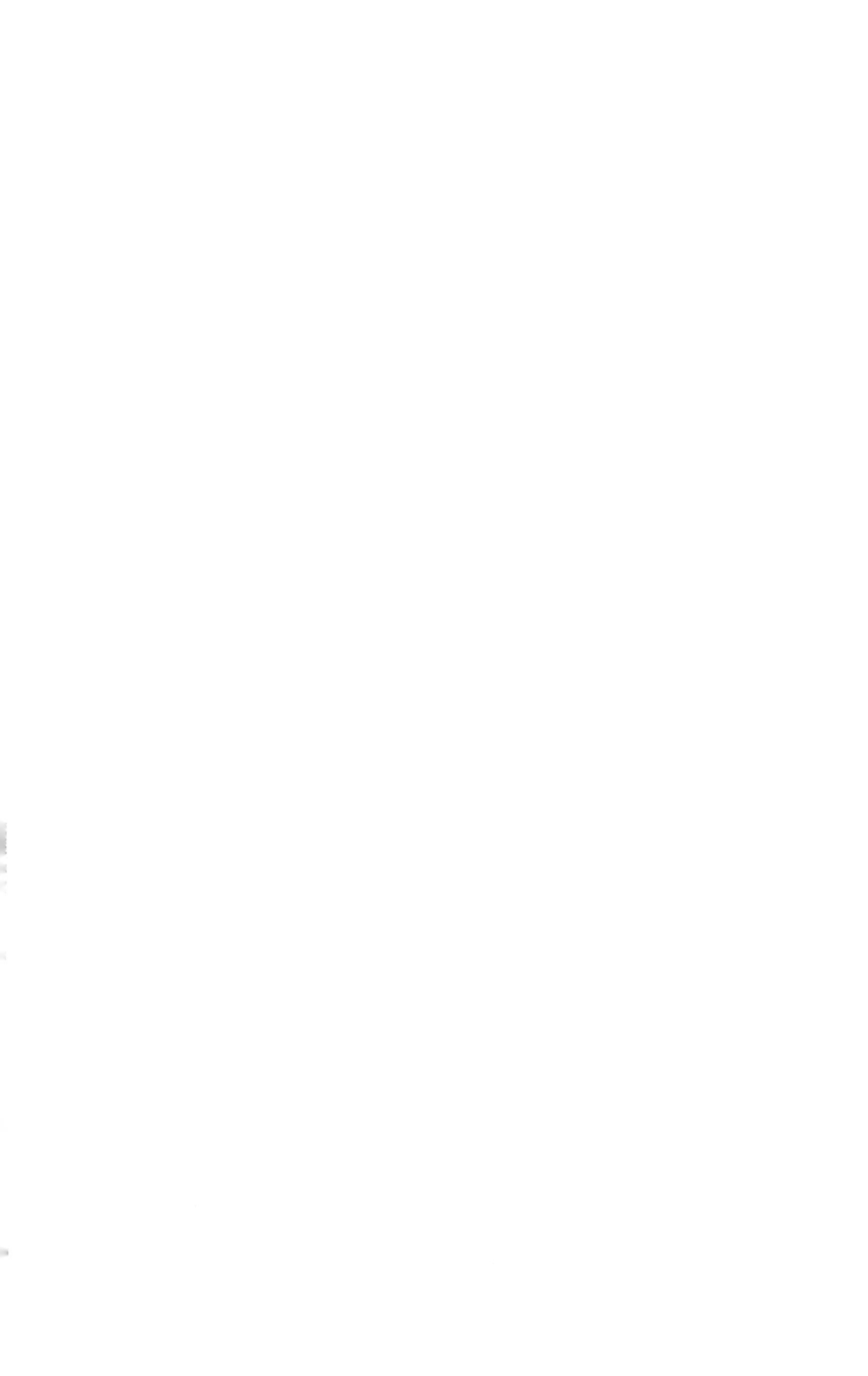